Average Anna

Jennifer Chandler

CHAPTER 1

Anna sat on the edge of the mat with her teammates, waiting for her score to be displayed. She had just competed on beam, her final event of the meet. Anna watched as her teammate Suryea began her beam routine, mounting the beam carefully. Suryea was so detail-oriented and focused. She always scored well.

Anna saw her score flash up: Anna Maddox—8.4. She sighed to herself. She tried her best, but somehow she never seemed to get much above an 8.5 on any event. Oh, occasionally she got an 8.6 or 8.7, but that was usually if the meet was an overall higher-scoring meet.

Kenzie tapped her shoulder. "I think that's at least a 9," she said, pointing to Suryea, who had just nailed her dismount.

"I agree," said Anna. She looked around at the other girls on the Xcel Silver team at Maple Hill Gymnastics. She thought most of them would probably go on to compete Xcel Gold next season. Except for her, it seemed like most of the other girls scored high regularly. Other than the fact that she occasionally fell, Anna wasn't sure why she didn't score better. She asked her coaches, and they tried to tell her how to fix her form and other issues. But this season had been average again. Just like last season and the season before that.

Anna clapped when a 9.25 flashed up on the scoreboard for Suryea. It had been a good routine; Suryea deserved that score.

Anna added up her scores on each apparatus in her head as the girls got their warm-ups on and prepared to go to the awards area. She started on floor with an 8.3. On vault, she scored an 8.55. Uneven bars had been an 8.1, and she had finished with the 8.4 on balance beam. It wasn't her worst meet ever. The all-around score was over 33. Not horrible, but not awesome.

Anna didn't figure she'd get any medals, but she always stayed for the awards to support her teammates. She was happy when a team member from the hosting gym brought over candy grams. Today her mom bought her a chocolate bar and a real rose. Anna's parents were always supportive, even though she wasn't the best-scoring gymnast in the world.

"How did you feel about the meet today?" Coach Cyndi interrupted her thoughts.

Anna swallowed her bite of the chocolate bar and then responded, "It was normal for me, I guess."

Coach Cyndi smiled and patted Anna on the shoulder. "Don't worry. Keep working hard, and you'll get there."

Anna hoped she was "getting there", but it didn't seem like it. She wanted to score 9s and get awards like the other girls on the team. She wanted to be more than average.

After the meet, she and her parents stopped for ice cream at Jane's Diner to celebrate.

"Good job today, honey," her dad said, as they sat outside the ice cream pick-up window on wooden benches.

"Thanks," said Anna, then changed the subject. "So I guess Reese went home today?"

It was a question that had an obvious answer, but Anna had to know for sure.

"He did," her mom nodded solemnly, "The social worker picked him up when you were on the way to the gym with Mrs. Carter. We left soon after that so we wouldn't miss your competition."

Anna's parents were foster parents. They usually took in one or two children at a time in the spare bedroom. They had been taking in foster kids for as long as Anna could remember, usually younger children and babies. Anna loved the children. They were a big part of her life, and whenever a child left to return home or to live with a relative, Anna felt sad.

"Did he cry?" asked Anna slowly.

"Yes. He did." Her mom wiped a tear from her eye as she answered Anna. "But Anna, he's back with his mom. And she worked hard to fulfill all the requirements to be able to take him home. So we should be happy for him and his mom and hope that it works out long-term."

Anna knew that sometimes it didn't work out long-term. Sometimes a foster child returned to

Anna's home. But she had to hope for the best for Reese.

Anna licked the last bit of ice cream out of the tiny piece of sugar cone that was left. "I wonder how long we'll have until we get a new child.

"I'm not sure," said her dad. "But I have a feeling it won't be long." There was a shortage of good foster homes in the area, and Anna considered her family to be one of the best.

Anna's mom was still finishing her water ice. Anna thought about gymnastics.

"I don't think I'll get to Xcel Gold next year," she said. "I'm not scoring high enough."

Anna's dad patted her back. "It's okay. You're still the best to us. We just want you to enjoy the sport and get exercise. You don't have to be the next Olympian."

Anna's mom agreed. "I'm just happy you found something you like to do!" she said.

Anna sighed, "But I do want to score better."

"Listen to what your coaches say, and I'm sure in time you will," said her dad.

Anna got up to throw her napkin away when her mom's phone rang. She peeked over as her mom picked it up to answer—it was the foster care agency. She was sure there was another foster child, maybe even two, coming to her house soon.

CHAPTER 2

There wasn't another foster child coming to Anna's house that day. It turned out that the agency just had a question for Anna's mom about Reese. Anna's dad pulled up in front of their house, and Anna grabbed her Maple Hill Gymnastics gym bag and headed for her bedroom.

Anna glanced in the mirror before taking off her leotard. Her brown hair was starting to come out of the bun that her mom had carefully fixed this morning. Anna removed the dark green bow and set it on her dresser. The house felt quiet without Reese here anymore. He had been boisterous and loud, but lots of fun. She sat on her bed for a moment, considering that just yesterday she had played basketball with him in the driveway. Today, he was gone.

"Anna?" she heard her mom's voice calling.

"I'm getting changed," Anna called from her room.

"I'm stripping Reese's bed now and taking the sheets and comforters to the washer. Can you set new bedding out when you're finished?" her mom asked.

"Sure!" called Anna. She quickly threw on sweatpants and a tie-dye t-shirt that said "Coal City Classic." She remembered that meet. She had scored over a 34; it was one of her better meets. Even though she was average at gymnastics, she still loved it. Most of her shirts were gymnastics-themed, usually from meets she had attended.

Anna left her bedroom and headed to the linen closet in the hallway. She wondered whether they would get a boy or a girl next. Or maybe even two boys or two girls. The bedroom they used for foster children was large and had two beds. She looked at the sheet selection. She decided on a springy-looking yellow and green plaid set. She took them out of the closet and placed them on the bare beds in the foster bedroom.

After that, Anna grabbed her competition leotard and walked to the kitchen and laundry room area.

Her mom would need to wash this leotard by hand so that the sequins would not fall off.

"Set that on top of the washer. I'll wash it next." Anna's mom instructed. She was seated at the kitchen table, enjoying a cup of coffee. "Do you want a cup of tea?"

"Yeah," said Anna. "I'll get it." She pulled her favorite box of blackberry tea out of the cupboard. "Where's dad?"

"Out mowing the lawn," said her mom. Anna's dad was an engineer. He was busy working on weekdays, so he always did the yard work on the weekends.

There was a knock at the door. Anna rushed over, hoping it was her friend and neighbor, Erica. She stood on her tiptoes and peeked through the window at the top of the door.

"Erica!" she said, opening the door.

"Can you come out? How was your meet? Did you get any medals?" Erica talked quickly.

"Go ahead out and play!" Anna's mom encouraged her.

Anna gulped down half her tea in one long drink and ran out the door.

"Where's Reese?" Erica asked as they made their way over to the swing set.

"He went to live with his mom," Anna said slowly.

Erica nodded. She had been friends with Anna for years and was used to the comings and goings of the many foster children Anna's family had hosted.

"Sorry. I'm sure you miss him. I will too." Erica said. "And how was your meet?"

"It was okay. I scored my usual." Anna said. "Sometimes I wonder if gymnastics is the sport for me. I love practicing, but I'm not good at it."

"You're way better at gymnastics than I am," Erica said. "Anyway, if you're enjoying it, who cares if you're winning. Get your bike, and let's ride for a while. We can go to the park."

"Okay," said Anna. "But first, let me tell my mom where we're going."

After Anna informed her mom and received permission, the two girls started off on their bikes. The early spring day was warmer than usual. Anna looked around at the other ranch houses on their street, all with the same manicured lawns and brick exteriors. She loved her section of Maple Hill.

At the park, the girls left their bikes by a tree and walked to the stream. The stream was beautiful, with the sun glinting on the water as it flowed over little pebbles and stones.

"Let's go wading," Anna suggested. They ventured in, and the water was frigid.

"Brr!" said Erica. "What were you thinking?"

Anna laughed. "I don't know." She went in a little deeper, letting the water numb her toes and legs.

"You're quiet today," said Erica.

"I miss Reese," said Anna. "And I'm worried for him. He was just getting used to living here with us. I hope his mom takes good care of him at home."

Suddenly, Anna felt a big splash of water on her back, and she turned to see Erica grinning. For a moment, she felt annoyed as the cold water soaked into her shirt, but then she decided to go ahead and join in, and she splashed Erica back as hard as she could.

Soon the two girls were sopping wet, laughing and shivering. They didn't stop right away, though, and just kept the splashing war going. Eventually, both of them were chilled to the bone. It was time to go home.

CHAPTER 3

Anna watched out the bus window, eagerly waiting for her stop. Unfortunately, they were still eight stops from her house. It was Monday, and school seemed long. She had math and English homework, but she couldn't bring herself to concentrate on the bus as everyone else was so loud.

Usually, Erica sat next to Anna, but Erica had left school early for a dentist appointment, so the seat beside her was empty. Anna rustled through her papers and pulled out the field trip permission slip her teacher had given her. It was for a class trip to Knoebel's Amusement Park. Anna couldn't wait! Usually, she went to Knoebel's with her family every summer, but going with Erica and her other friends at school would make it even more fun.

When the bus stopped, Anna skipped into the house, hoping maybe her mom had made cookies that afternoon. Sometimes, if her mom had free time, she would make a batch of brown sugar cookies, which were Anna's favorite. Her mom's peanut butter bar cookies were pretty tasty also.

When Anna walked in, her mom was in the kitchen on the phone, writing things down on a piece of paper. She looked deep in the midst of a conversation, so Anna decided to put her things away. She ran to her room and set her books on her desk. Anna glanced at her gymnastics medal hanger on the wall. It was not very full. In fact, she had only won eight medals so far in all of Xcel Bronze and Xcel Silver.

Anna sighed and turned to her leotard selection, also hanging on hooks on her bedroom wall. She wasn't sure whether she wanted to wear her dark blue leotard or her pink leotard today. Finally, she decided on the pink leotard. Anna pulled it on and arranged her straight brown hair into a high bun. She pulled on a pair of bar shorts, and she was ready for gymnastics practice.

Anna still had another hour until she left for practice. She considered doing her homework but decided to save it for later. She unlocked her cupboard and pulled out her pile of sewing patterns, placing the stack on her bed. Anna had to keep everything locked up in her room that might be dangerous, like her sewing machine, scissors, needles, and other sewing supplies. Because her family cared for foster children, it was important to keep anything remotely dangerous locked safely away.

Anna's grandmother had taught her how to sew a couple summers ago, and Anna had practiced ever since. Even though not a lot of girls she knew enjoyed sewing, Anna found it relaxing. She often sewed in her spare time. She sometimes went to yard sales with her mom on Saturdays to look for sewing patterns. Other times, she purchased them online, using funds from her allowance.

Anna held up the pattern for a pillowcase. This was the last thing she had sewn—a pillowcase for Reese. She had let him pick out the fabric online. Reese loved airplanes, so he picked a flannel fabric adorned with various aircraft. Anna was glad she had time to finish sewing the pillowcase before Reese went home with his mom. Her mom had washed it and packed it for him to take home. Anna liked sewing things for the children that came to stay with them.

Anna picked up a pattern for a summer dress. This dress pattern was a simple sundress that had been designed in the 1970s, but Anna had seen that these dresses were coming back in style. She would like to sew herself this sundress to wear to the gymnastics banquet and award night in May. She pulled out the instructions for the pattern and soon confirmed that it was one she could sew easily. She just needed to pick the perfect fabric.

Picking up her Chromebook from school, Anna pulled up the browser and found her favorite fabric website. She quickly glanced through the new options they were advertising for spring and summer. A pretty linen with tiny purple and yellow flowers immediately caught her eye. It looked like it would be perfect for her sundress.

"Anna!" her mom called, "Come get some food before practice." Anna usually ate a light dinner before she left for practice since she wouldn't be home until after 8:00 p.m.

"Coming!" Anna quickly put the patterns back into her sewing cupboard and locked it. She grabbed her gym bag and ran out to the dining room. Her mom had a ham and cheese sandwich and some carrot sticks waiting on a plate.

"I think I'm going to sew a dress for the gymnastics awards banquet," Anna told her mom as she ate.

"That's a wonderful idea. Do you have a pattern?" her mom asked.

Anna nodded. "One I bought last year at the yard sale at the community center."

"Nice!" her mom smiled encouragingly. "Don't forget to fill up your water bottle before we leave for the gym."

"Don't worry. I'll remember," said Anna, grabbing another carrot.

Chapter 4

Maple Hill Gymnastics felt like a second home to Anna. She started mommy-and-me classes at age 3, preschool classes at 4, and moved to preteam at 6. When she was 8, Anna started competing Xcel Bronze. Two-and-a-half years later, she moved to the Xcel Silver team. Now, at age 12, she was still Xcel Silver. Meanwhile, during all those years, her coaches and teammates had become close, almost like family.

Anna put her slides in her cubby and waved across the gym to Suryea and Kenzie, who were already in line for the warm-up. Coach Cyndi walked by just then. "Hey, Anna, how are you?"

Anna smiled. "Good," she said. "How are you?"

Coach Cyndi laughed. "It was a long day. I took my dog to a new dog groomer. The pet groomer was great, but Cookie just hates the process."

Anna nodded. "Well, I'm sure she looks great." She knew Coach Cyndi loved Cookie.

The girls did their warm-ups and went to start out on beam. Eventually, Coach Cyndi assigned them to work on cartwheels. Anna found them frustrating because she kept falling off the side of the beam. She didn't understand how Suryea and Kenzie could land cartwheels so easily.

Coach Cyndi had her go over to the low beam so she could spot Anna. She helped Anna get into the right body position, then spotted her and assisted her in actually landing on the beam. Anna was happy that she was able to land the cartwheels with Coach Cyndi's help but a little frustrated because it seemed to be taking her so much time and effort compared to her teammates.

Anna kept working hard, and eventually, she was able to land a cartwheel occasionally on the low beam. "Now we need to work on getting your form better. Toes pointed, knees straight," Coach Cyndi reminded her.

At break, Anna and Kenzie were about to sit down to eat their snack when one of the boys, Tyree, ran over to them.

"We're all doing our routines to practice for our state competition next week," he said. "Do you want to come over and watch?"

Anna and Kenzie looked at each other and shrugged. "Sure," they said together.

Anna grabbed her granola bar and took a large bite before she headed over to the boys' section of the gym. Maple Hill Gymnastics was split into different sections: the preschool section, the trampoline area, the girls' section, and the boys' section. It looked like the boys' team was going to start out with their high bar routines.

Anna watched as the first boy saluted the coach the way he would salute a judge before he started his routine. One of the other boy's coaches lifted him to the high bar. He began his routine with a pullover. This boy's routine was basic, finishing with a tucked flyaway. Anna didn't know that much about boys' gymnastics, but she guessed that he was a level 3 or 4.

Everyone clapped when he finished, and the next boy got ready to perform his routine. Anna liked when she got a chance to watch the boys. They seemed to have a lot of fun while still taking their gymnastics seriously. They enthusiastically cheered each other on as they competed, and they displayed a lot of team spirit.

After watching a few more easy routines, a taller boy stood up and got ready to do his routine. Anna couldn't remember his name, but then she heard one of his teammates shout. "Go, Jared!"

Jared swung into giants right away when he mounted the bar, and then he did a move where he let go of the bar and did a flip, then caught the bar again. Everyone cheered and clapped. Jared was really good; Anna figured he must be a level 10. He finished his routine with a dismount that involved multiple twists. Jared took a big step on the landing, but other than that, his routine was amazing.

"Girls, let's get back to practice!" Anna heard Coach Cyndi's voice. She motioned them over towards the uneven bars. Anna stopped watching the boys' team and ran to her cubby to put her snack bag away. Kenzie was right behind her.

"Do you think you'll ever be as good at gymnastics as those boys are?" she asked Kenzie.

"I don't know. I plan to hopefully go to Xcel Gold next year." Kenzie answered seriously. "I am guessing some of them, like Jared, are just naturally talented."

"Maybe," Anna said.

"Maybe they just work hard," Suryea said. "My dad always says that hard work can often beat out talent if talent doesn't work hard," she repeated the quote casually.

Anna sighed. She felt as if she did work hard in gymnastics. But she still wasn't winning. She remained average. She walked over to the uneven bars, determined to work even harder than ever.

CHAPTER 5

"How was practice?" asked Anna's mom as she got into the car after practice.

Anna shrugged. "Normal, I guess." Her mom always asked about practice, but sometimes Anna didn't feel like talking about it, especially if she felt discouraged or like she wasn't making progress.

Anna's mom pulled into Jane's Diner. "How about some ice cream?"

Anna was surprised. They normally didn't stop for ice cream after practice on a school night, but she was never one to turn down a delicious ice cream cone.

Anna sat across from her mom at the picnic table, glad she had her jacket on as the spring nights were still cool in Pennsylvania. She licked the black raspberry ice cream and watched her mom take a bite of rainbow sherbet.

"I wanted to let you know that we'll be getting two new girls while you're at school tomorrow," her mom said suddenly, looking at Anna.

Anna felt a bit of excitement. She had wondered when the next child or children would arrive.

"Really?" Anna said, "What are their names? What did the agency tell you about them?"

"The older girl is six years old. She'll be going to Kindergarten on the bus with you as soon as we can get her enrolled. Her name is Sparrow." Anna's mom replied. "Her sister Fern is only two years old. They're coming from a home where they lived with their mom and a lot of other different people. Things have been very chaotic for them. This is the second time they've been in foster care."

Anna nodded. Her mom usually gave her some basic background information. She didn't give Anna a whole lot of detail about the children they were fostering. A lot of it was confidential or personal information.

"I cleaned the bedroom again today," Anna's mom continued. "And Dad moved one of the beds out and replaced it with a crib. Fern still sleeps in a crib. I went to the store and picked out a few clothing items, but we'll see what else the girls need when they arrive."

Anna knew her mom would already have the essentials ready for any foster children that came to stay at her home. She kept lots of brand-new toothbrushes, toothpaste, diapers, soap, packages of new underwear in many sizes, shampoo, hair brushes, and other essentials in the hallway cupboard. That way, they were always prepared when new children arrived.

Anna was aware that her mom would take the girls to shop for clothes as soon as possible and register the older one for school. Typically, the girls would have many medical and dental appointments and possibly visitation with their parent/parents.

Anna's parents were really dedicated to being the best foster parents they could be, and Anna admired what they did. Sometimes, she did feel a little bit like the foster kids came first, and she struggled with those feelings. Other times, she struggled because she wanted to do something but her parents were busy with the foster children—at an appointment or visitation.

But she knew her parents loved her, and her parents tried to make that very clear. They spent time with her often, gave her as many opportunities as they could, and tried their best to attend any school and gymnastics events that she had.

When they arrived home, Anna ran to put her gymnastics bag in her bedroom. Then she went next door to the room where the new foster girls would be staying. She noted how prepared the room already was! The bedding was clean and inviting, and toiletries were already out on the dresser, along with fresh towels and washcloths.

Anna made her way back to her own bedroom and changed out of her leotard and gym shorts. She chose her black and white polka-dot flannel pajamas and slid her feet into her fur-lined slippers.

Plopping on her bed, Anna picked up her journal. She liked to write about the foster kids they cared for so that she would always remember them, even after they went home. Basically, she realized that her journal mostly consisted of stories about her gymnastics adventures mixed with stories about her family's foster care experiences. She turned to the last page she had written—that was the day that Reese had gone home.

Glancing at the wall, Anna looked at her family picture on the wall of her, her mom, and her dad. She once asked her parents why they didn't have any more kids after they had her. Anna's mom said they had purposely decided to care for foster children instead of having more kids of their own. Anna was okay with that mostly, but sometimes she wished she had a brother or sister.

The next picture on the wall was a gymnastics chalk portrait. Maple Hill Gymnastics had done chalk gymnastics pictures last year, and it had been a lot of fun. Anna loved the way it turned out. She looked fabulous in her team leo, surrounded by the multi-colored chalk effects. If only, she thought, she was a better gymnast. She needed to keep working and keep trying. Maybe someday she'd be good and not average.

CHAPTER 6

The cafeteria at Maple Hill Elementary seemed louder than usual. Erica plopped down next to Anna and pulled out her lunch.

"Ughh," Erica complained. "I should have packed my own lunch. Whenever I don't, my mom tells my older brother to pack for me. He gave me a dry ham sandwich. I bet he puts mustard on his sandwiches. He's so annoying."

Anna shrugged and pulled out leftover pizza. "I should heat this up," she said. She glanced at the line for the microwave, where at least twenty students were waiting. "On second thought," she added, "Cold pizza really isn't that bad after all."

Just then, two boys from Anna's class sat down by Anna and Erica. Anna felt annoyed as soon as she saw them sit down. Kevin and Shane were the most irritating boys in her entire grade. Why were they sitting here today? She had been hoping for a quiet lunch with Erica.

"Look what my uncle sent me," Kevin announced right away. He dug into his lunch sack.

And pulled out a plastic pouch of something. Anna eyed up the label. "Crunchy Edible Mixed Bugs", it read.

Anna felt sick. She nudged Erica. "Edible mixed bugs," she whispered. "They're about to eat them."

"What kind of bugs are in there?" Shane asked.

Kevin held up the package, glancing over to see if the girls were watching. Anna knew she should ignore them, but she and Erica just couldn't seem to look away.

"Crickets, grasshoppers, and Sago Worms," he read. "Highly nutritious and packed full of vitamins, minerals, and proteins."

"Yep. Deeeeeelicious!" Kevin said in an exaggerated tone of voice. "Girls, would you like to try one?" He looked right at Anna.

"I'm not touching that. It's nasty," she said.

Kevin laughed. "Shane, I'll give you $5 if you try one of each."

Shane hesitated, then slowly took the bag from Kevin. He looked into the bag tentatively. Gingerly, he reached his hand inside and pulled out a grasshopper, holding it up for everyone to see. Anna felt her stomach turn.

"It doesn't look bad," Kevin said. "Seriously, I bet it tastes no different than your favorite crunchy potato chip or maybe a pretzel. Come on now. Five dollars is waiting for you, Shane."

"I bet it tastes a lot different than my favorite potato chips," whispered Erica to Anna.

Anna nodded. "I agree," she whispered back.

"Let's go to the bathroom," said Erica. "I can't watch this." The two girls got up and quickly went to the restroom.

"Boys are disgusting sometimes," Anna complained. "Ughhh. Who brings bugs to school for lunch?"

"Yeah," said Erica as she washed her hands.

"We're getting two new girls to live with us, starting today while I'm at school." Anna changed the subject as she pulled off a paper towel to dry her hands.

"Oh wow, two girls. That's cool. What are their names?" Erica replied.

The two girls left the restroom and walked back to their spots at the table. "Sparrow is six years old, and Fern is two," Anna explained. "Sparrow will ride the bus with us once my mom has her registered for school."

The boys had put the bugs away by the time the girls reached their seats, and Anna felt relieved. She grabbed her bag of apple slices, hoping she had time to finish them before the bell rang.

Erica picked up her ham sandwich and took a big bite. All of a sudden, Anna heard Shane and Kevin start laughing. They were looking at Erica. And Erica's face suddenly turned pale.

Erica got up from her seat before Anna knew what was happening and ran to the trash can as fast as she could possibly go.

"Walk!" said a lunch monitor, but Erica did not comply. She got to the trash can and spit everything out. She looked deathly sick.

Anna turned to the boys, realization hitting her. "You put a bug in her sandwich!" she said angrily. "What's wrong with you? Now you'll get in trouble." She saw Erica talking to the teacher, still looking pale and sick.

"I don't care if we get in trouble," Kevin retorted. "It was so fun watching that." He and Shane started laughing again.

Anna hurried over to make sure Erica was okay. She looked like she was about to cry. Mrs. Karnam, one of the teachers, was patting her back.

"I'm going to talk to those boys right now," she was saying. "They'll certainly face consequences for this."

"Are you okay?" Anna asked Erica.

Erica nodded. "I'm just still feeling a little sick. I think it was a cricket. It crunched like one."

Anna felt queasy thinking about it. "Sorry, Erica," she said. "Let's make sure we're not sitting near Kevin or Shane tomorrow."

Erica nodded. "Okay," she said. One of the lunch ladies brought her another drink of water. Anna couldn't wait until school was over for the day.

Chapter 7

Anna heard a young child crying when she walked into her house. The sound was coming from the bedroom area. Anna quickly ran down the hallway to her own room and dumped her backpack on the floor. She noticed the door to the foster bedroom was open, and she could hear her mom's voice speaking softly in the midst of the cries.

Sometimes it went smoothly when new foster children arrived. Other times, it was tough. Anna's parents had explained to Anna that it was a huge adjustment for these children. First, they were taken out of their own home. Even if they were being treated badly, they still missed their parents or caregivers. It was hard for Anna to understand completely, but she trusted what her parents said.

Now the children were in an entirely different environment than what they were used to. The people were new, the surroundings were new, and the town was new. Sometimes the children came from the city, and Anna thought Maple Hill must really seem different to them.

Anna ventured out of her bedroom and peeked into the bedroom next door. A little girl with brown hair, still wet from a bath or shower, was sitting quietly on the bed, staring into space. That must be Sparrow. The crying was coming from another little girl, a toddler, who had clearly been bathed and put into fresh, new clothing. She was clutching a rather dirty stuffed bear, and murmuring "Mama" between sobs.

Anna's mom sat on the floor next to her, speaking soothing words. Anna stepped into the room hesitantly. Anna's mom looked up.

"Oh hey, Anna! You're home." She glanced at her watch. "I didn't realize it was that late already." Anna's mom turned to the girls.

"Anna, this is Sparrow," she said, gesturing to the girl on the bed. Anna smiled and gave a quick wave. "Hi,

Sparrow." Sparrow didn't smile at all, but she waved back.

"And this is Fern," Anna's mom continued, motioning toward the crying two-year-old.

"Hi, I'm Anna." Anna knelt down and smiled at the little girl. "It's nice to meet you."

Fern stopped crying for a moment. She looked at Anna with wide eyes. "Mama," she said again, without crying.

Anna moved towards the closet and brought out a big basket of toys that would be age-appropriate for Fern. She was glad her parents always kept these on hand; she usually helped her dad wash and dry them between foster placements.

"Here, Fern," Anna said, "Look at these." She pulled out a container of large blocks that snapped together and began to build. Fern just continued staring at Anna. "Let's make a castle." Anna continued.

Anna continued building, and then she saw another hand come up from behind and pick up a block. Sparrow had grown interested and was helping her build. Anna's mom joined in, but Fern still kept a wary distance.

"Come help us." Sparrow finally said to Fern, speaking the first words Anna had heard her speak. Hesitantly, Fern joined them, stuffed animal still in one hand. She sat quietly next to Sparrow and began to hand blocks to her sister. Soon they had a good-sized castle built. They all sat back and admired it.

Anna's mom looked at her watch again. "Girls," she said, "Let's pick up the blocks we aren't using and go outside. Anna has to get ready for gymnastics practice now." The girls nodded. Fern seemed to have stopped crying for the time being. Anna's mom took her hand, and Sparrow followed them down the hallway, toward the living room.

Anna went back to her bedroom and picked a swirled, multicolored leotard from her leotard rack. This one was one of her favorites because the material was so soft and cozy. She knew the new foster girls would have plenty to do with her mom in the backyard. There were tricycles to ride on the patio, a swing set, and a sandbox. They also had a deck box full of balls and other outdoor toys.

Picking up her hairbrush, Anna decided on braids today for practice. She easily put her long, brown hair into two braids – her mom taught her how to braid when she was six years old. After she finished getting ready for gymnastics, Anna picked up her gym bag. She left her bedroom, then hesitated. She turned and went back into the foster bedroom.

Anna looked around. It didn't appear that the girls had brought much with them. She knew her mom would wash almost everything right away. Sometimes kids showed up at Anna's house with nothing. Other times, they brought all that they had in garbage bags. Anna thought it was sad that some children didn't even own a suitcase. Anna's parents never let a foster child leave their home without brand-new luggage.

Outside, Anna's mom was pushing Fern on the baby swing. Fern was smiling and looked like she was enjoying it. Sparrow was riding a tricycle. She ran over to Anna.

"You do gymnastics?" she asked. Anna was surprised.

"Yes, I do," she said and smiled at the little girl.

"I always wanted to do gymnastics," Sparrow said eagerly. She talked with maturity, sounding older than her six years. "Can you teach me how to do a cartwheel?"

Anna nodded, "Of course," she said, "I can't do it right now because I have to go to practice, but maybe on the weekend."

"Oh, thank you!" Sparrow sounded excited. "Can you teach me dance too?"

"I'll teach you any dance moves I know," Anna promised.

"Anna, grab your snack and water bottle while I put the girls in the van." her mom instructed.

"Okay," Anna replied and headed back inside.

CHAPTER 8

Anna waved goodbye to both girls when she got out of the van. She liked them both already and looked forward to playing more with them. She wondered why they had been put in foster care, but she knew that wasn't her business. Her mom and dad knew, but that information was confidential. Anna really wished people would just treat their children with kindness and love.

"Tonight, we'll be doing a routine night." Coach Cyndi announced. "After warm-up, each girl will do five routines on every event." Anna liked routine nights. It gave her a chance to work on getting her routines more smooth. She knew she needed to improve her form and perfect the details, and routine nights gave her an opportunity to work hard at that. In gymnastics, every movement mattered!

The girls moved to their first event, the uneven bars. Anna didn't wear grips yet. Usually, Coach Cyndi recommended grips after they learned their kips. Anna had been working on her kip during skills upgrade practice times, but she still didn't have it. When they did drills to help the girls learn kips, Anna felt like those were helping. Why didn't she have her kip yet? Suryea and Kenzie already had their kips. It was frustrating.

Anna chalked up her hands carefully.

"I hate routine nights," Kenzie complained while they stood around the chalk bucket. "I can't wait until the season is over and I can start working Gold routines and skills all the time."

Anna hesitated, then said, "I still need to practice my routines."

"I want to do well at the state championship," Suryea said. "I finished sixth last year, and I'm hoping to place higher this year."

Anna felt as if she would never place at the state level. She rarely got a medal at regular meets, let alone at the state meet. Oh well, it wasn't just about the medals, she told herself—it was about improvement and doing the best she could. That's what her parents always told her.

Coach Cyndi nodded for Anna to start her routine. Anna began with her pullover. She tried to focus on keeping her legs straight and her toes pointed. Then, she did a cast, followed by a back hip circle in quick succession. She finished her bars routine with an underswing dismount.

"The pullover was excellent," Coach Cyndi commented. "Your legs were tighter and straighter than I've seen in a while. Now, you could definitely improve on the height of your cast, and you landed a bit short on the dismount. See if you can improve those things in your next routine."

Anna nodded and got back in line. She had been doing this same routine for two years now. She glanced over and saw some of the optional gymnasts practicing on floor. One of the girls ran and did a beautiful double back tuck.

"I hope I can do that someday," Anna said to Suryea, who had also been watching.

"I do back tucks on my trampoline at home." Suryea stated, "But I can't do even one back tuck on the floor here. Not yet. I'm getting closer, though."

Anna's following routines improved a little bit each time, and Anna felt satisfied that at least she had made some progress. The girls moved to floor next.

All the Xcel Silver girls liked the peppy music Coach Cyndi had selected for their floor routine. In Xcel Bronze and Xcel Silver, the girls at Maple Hill Gymnastics competed the same routine. It wasn't until Xcel Gold that the gymnasts were able to pick their own music.

Anna was first in line to practice. She got into her starting pose and waited for Coach Cyndi to start the music. She heard the familiar strains and began her first dance steps. Soon, she was doing her cartwheel, backward roll combo. She did her split leap next and her full turn. Finally, she finished with her final pass which included a front handspring, forward roll.

"Anna, that was beautiful!" Coach Cyndi said. "That was one of the best routines on floor that I've seen you do this year."

Anna was surprised. She had felt like the routine had gone smoothly, but she didn't realize it was that good. "Really?" she asked Coach Cyndi.

"Definitely," the coach nodded. "Now, you need to work on your hand position in some of your dance moves. We'll go over that. Also, your legs weren't completely straight in your split leap. The judges always notice that and take a deduction." Coach Cyndi then showed her where her hands should be placed at different times throughout the routine.

After the other girls had taken their turns, it was time for break. Anna, Kenzie, and Suryea were glad it was warm enough to take their break outside.

Kenzie held up her brown paper bag. "I literally lost two lunch boxes at school this year," she said in exasperation. "My mom is so annoyed. So for now I have to use paper bags until I can do enough chores to earn a new one."

Suryea nodded. "My mom would be annoyed too."

"We got new foster kids," said Anna. The girls turned to her, interested.

"Really? Boys or girls?" asked Kenzie.

Anna eagerly told them what she knew about the new girls who had come to stay at her home. "They seem so sweet," she said, "I can't wait to play with them more. Sparrow wants to learn gymnastics and dance."

"That's so cool," said Kenzie. "I wish my family could do that. I asked my mom a while ago, but she said she has enough on her plate right now."

"I understand that," said Anna as she bit into an apple slice. "My parents are really busy with appointments and just taking care of the foster kids. It's hard sometimes for them, I think."

Kenzie, Anna, and Suryea put their snack bags away and went to beam, which would be their next event.

CHAPTER 9

A few nights later, Anna was startled awake in the middle of the night. She had been dreaming, and it wasn't a good dream. She had dreamed she was at a gymnastics competition, and the floor music started playing. But in her dream, instead of doing her routine, Anna just stood there. She had forgotten how to begin her routine. She had looked over at the judges, and the looks on their faces had been very disapproving. Then she sat up in bed and woke up. She looked at the time on her alarm clock—2:00 a.m. It was way too early to be awake!

Anna was glad that it was just a dream! She was about to tuck herself back under her quilt when she heard crying. It wasn't coming from the bedroom next door. Anna got out of bed and slid her feet into her fuzzy slippers. She cracked open her door and listened. It was definitely coming from the living room. Cautiously, Anna stepped out into the hall and tiptoed toward the living room.

In the corner of the living room, Anna's mom sat with Fern wrapped in a fluffy blanket on her lap, rocking her slowly and singing a song. Fern was holding her stuffed animal tightly to herself. She was sobbing and saying "Mama".

How heartbreaking, thought Anna. Despite whatever had happened in Fern's home that was the cause of her removal, Fern clearly missed her mother desperately. Anna understood more why her mom thought it was really good when a birth parent worked hard at all their goals for reunification. Her parents always seemed happy when a parent wanted to do the right thing and work to be reunited with their child.

Anna stood there for five minutes, just watching her mom rock Fern and tenderly sing to her. She loved her mom a lot at that moment because she saw again how patient, tender, and caring she was. Anna's mom treated Anna that way also, and Anna appreciated it. Here her mom was, at 2:00 a.m., lovingly singing to a sorrowful and lonely child. Anna stored up the memory in her mind and tiptoed back to her room. She hoped that Fern would be consoled soon.

On Saturday, Anna was finishing her breakfast when Erica knocked on her front door. Anna ran to open it and told Erica to come in.

"Can I meet Sparrow and Fern?" she asked eagerly.

Anna shook her head. "My mom took them for an appointment, and then there's another meeting with their social worker. They won't be back for several hours."

"Oh," Erica sounded disappointed. "Let's go outside and do something."

"My dad's working on something out back. I'll ask him if that's okay." Anna said, putting her cereal bowl and spoon into the dishwasher.

After getting her dad's permission to go outside, Anna and Erica got on their bikes and rode leisurely down Anna's street. Suddenly, Anna heard someone call her name. "Anna!"

She turned around. It was Parker, a boy from gymnastics. Anna didn't know him well, but she waved. He and his dad were in the backyard, starting a fire in their fire pit. Anna and Erica got off their bikes and slowly wheeled them to the edge of Parker's fence.

"Hey, Parker, isn't it a little early in the morning for a campfire?" asked Anna, then added, "This is Erica, my friend from school. Erica, this is Parker from gymnastics. He's a level. . " she paused. "What level are you, Parker?"

"Level 6 this year," Parker said. "Hi, Erica. Nice to meet you. I've seen you around on your bike."

"Do you go to our school?" asked Erica. "We're in sixth grade."

"I'm in sixth grade too," Parker explained. "But I homeschool. I love it. It gives me a lot of time for other things."

Anna nodded. "I have other friends who are homeschooled," she said.

"Do you want to come in? My dad said it's okay. We're about to fry some eggs and sausage over the fire." Parker said.

Anna used Erica's phone to call her dad after Erica had called her mom. They both got permission to join Parker and his dad at their fire. Parker's dad had a heavy-duty skillet that fit perfectly over the campfire. He waited until the fire had died down to put the skillet on top.

Parker cracked the first couple of eggs. "Do you want to crack a few?" Parker's dad asked the girls. Anna eagerly volunteered.

"I crack them all the time at home when my mom is baking," Anna explained. She carefully cracked five more eggs into the skillet.

Parker's dad opened a package of sausage. "This will add some flavor," he explained.

Erica sprinkled salt and pepper on top of the eggs. Everything sizzled nicely in the frying pan, and the smell was delicious.

While the food was finishing, Anna, Erica, and Parker went over to Parker's swing set. His dad had designed and built it himself when Parker was younger, and there was a pullover bar at the end. They had a great time practicing pullovers and casts. Parker was pretty good at everything—he even did a flyaway off the bar. Anna was impressed.

The eggs and sausage were delicious! Parker's dad had cooked just the right amount for each of them to have a nice-sized serving. When they had finished eating, Anna and Erica decided to ride their bikes around town for a little while longer. Parker had chores to finish, so they said goodbye to him as they headed off.

"That was fun," said Erica. "I love Saturdays."

Anna agreed.

CHAPTER 10

When Erica met Sparrow and Fern later, she immediately fell in love with the girls. They were in the backyard playing under Anna's mom's watchful eye. Sparrow ran over to Anna immediately.

"Can you teach me gymnastics and dance now?" she asked.

"Of course," said Anna, then motioned towards Erica. "Sparrow, this is Erica. Erica, meet Sparrow."

Erica smiled and waved. "I love your name," she said to Sparrow. "It's beautiful!"

"My mom named me that," Sparrow said quietly. "She loves to be outside, and she said she likes names that remind her of nature."

Erica nodded. "That's so cool," she said.

Anna introduced Erica to Fern, who didn't take much notice and kept riding a tricycle around the patio.

"Okay, Sparrow, do you know any gymnastics?" Anna asked.

Sparrow bent over and did a forward roll into the grass. Erica clapped.

"That's great!" Anna exclaimed. "Now let me help you do another one. This time we'll keep your feet together and start with your hands in this position." Anna did a forward roll herself to show Sparrow what she meant.

Sparrow tried another forward roll.

"Wow, Sparrow," said Anna. "That was a big improvement. Keep trying!"

They practiced forward rolls while Erica went over to throw a ball with Fern, who was done riding the tricycle. After that, Anna taught her a few of the easier dance moves and positions she knew. At Maple Hill Gymnastics, all the girls had dance class once a week. The coaches said that would help them improve their scores, especially on floor.

Sparrow was quite eager to learn as much as she could, and Anna wished she could take her to gymnastics class. She felt as if Sparrow would learn a lot more if she had all the proper equipment to learn on, as well as good coaching. She decided to talk to her mom about it later, in private.

That night, after the girls had gone to bed, Anna opened the package that had arrived that day. It was the fabric she had ordered on the website—the fabric with the beautiful tiny purple and yellow flowers. She couldn't wait to start sewing the dress for her gymnastics award night and banquet. She fingered the fabric softly; then she stood up and held it up to her in front of the mirror, imagining how she would look in the dress she was going to make.

Anna loved the way the fabric looked in the lighting, against her face. It seemed to go perfectly with her brown hair and skin tones. She couldn't wait to get started on the dress. Anna unlocked her sewing cupboard and pulled out the dress pattern. She removed the instructions from the package and started reading. It didn't look too hard at all. She was sure she could finish sewing it in time for the banquet.

Anna's mom knocked on the door, "Can I come in?"

"Sure," said Anna.

When Anna's mom entered the room, Anna showed her the dress fabric and the pattern.

"That's really stunning," Anna's mom said. "I love the combination of that fabric with this vintage pattern. And this style has really come back within the last year. You'll look great at the banquet in that!"

Anna smiled. "I hope so," she said. She paused for a moment, "Mom, do you think we could take Sparrow to Maple Hill Gymnastics for classes? They have beginner classes for her age, and I know she'd really love it."

Anna's mom thought for a moment, "That's a good idea, Anna. I would have to check with her social worker and see how we would work it out. I may need her mom's permission. The next time I talk to Mrs. Lim from the agency, we'll discuss if it's a possibility."

"Oh good. Thanks, Mom," Anna smiled.

"How's school going?" asked her mom. She always tried to make sure she spent plenty of one-on-one time with Anna. Anna knew her parents wanted her to know how important she was to them.

Sometimes things got busy with the foster children, but Anna knew her parents loved her and cared for her.

"It's okay. Oh yeah. . " Anna grabbed a piece of paper off her desk. "I have a field trip permission form for you to sign. We're going to Knoebel's Amusement Park soon. I can't wait!" Anna handed her mom the paper.

Picking up a pen from the desk, Anna's mom signed the form, then read through the information. "This looks like lots of fun," she commented.

"It will be great to go with Erica," Anna added. "We both love roller coasters, so that's probably what we'll do most of the day!"

Anna felt satisfied as she went to sleep that night. She had a field trip to look forward to, a beautiful dress to sew, and her mom was looking into gymnastics lessons for Sparrow.

Chapter 11

The following Saturday was the annual Spring Fest at Maple Hill Gymnastics. All the gymnasts looked forward to this annual fundraising event. The parking lot was full of food options, games, and even a live band. Anna's favorite food there was the smoked barbecue chicken. One of the dads from the boys' team had his own special recipe, and he donated the chicken every year. It usually sold out quickly.

Inside, the gymnasts would take turns showcasing their skills according to a set schedule. Anna knew that the Xcel Silvers would do some skills on each event at 1:00 p.m. This was a chance for Maple Hill community members to come inside and see what Maple Hill Gymnastics was all about. The preschool area of the gym was open for free play.

Anna's mom dropped her off at 9:00 a.m. The gymnasts were welcome to hang out all day and help. Anna's parents would come later on to have lunch and watch her perform. Anna was looking forward to showing Sparrow and Fern around the gym. She was excited that they would be able to play in the preschool area, try out the equipment, and meet some of her gymnastic friends.

Kenzie was at the dunking booth, throwing a ball to try to dunk Coach Michelle, one of the compulsory coaches. She missed and looked disappointed. Anna ran over.

"Hey Kenzie!" she waved. "Has anyone been able to dunk her yet? She looks dry."

"Not yet," said Kenzie sadly.

Just then, Charlotte, Preslie, and Tyree walked over together.

"I saw you miss," said Tyree, who was on the boys' team. "Now watch the expert." He dug out three crumpled one-dollar bills from the pocket of his athletic shorts. Coach Jennifer, who was handling the money, handed him a basket of ten balls.

"Here goes," said Tyree. He pulled out the first ball, aimed, and watched as the ball took flight. It missed the mark.

"Ha!" said Kenzie. "You missed too."

"But you missed with ten balls," Tyree said as he picked up another one. He aimed, threw, and missed again.

"Can I try?" asked Anna.

"I don't know," said Tyree. "I only have eight more balls."

"Please," Anna begged. She didn't even think she'd make it, but she wanted to try just one throw. And she really didn't want to spend $3.

"Oh, okay," said Tyree reluctantly, passing her a ball.

Anna picked up the ball, aimed, and threw.

Splash! Everyone watched in shock. Somehow, the ball had found its mark right in the middle of the target, and down into the dunk tank fell Coach Michelle!

For a moment, they were all so surprised that no one reacted. Then they all clapped and cheered.

"Go, Anna!" said Preslie. "That was awesome."

Anna felt happy as they all congratulated her, and Tyree gave her a high five. She couldn't believe she had actually hit the target. As she watched Tyree throw more balls, her mind drifted for a moment. She wondered suddenly if the feeling she had now was the feeling of being a winner.

She had often thought about how it would feel to actually win a gymnastics competition someday. Maybe this happy feeling was it. It was the feeling of success. It was the feeling of being more than average, for a change.

Splash! Again, Coach Michelle fell into the tank. Tyree had hit the target again with his final ball, and everyone cheered once more.

"Finally!" he said. "I finally hit it!"

He handed the empty basket back to Coach Jennifer.

"What should we do now?" asked Charlotte.

"Let's go play skeeball," said Kenzie.

They ran over to the skeeball, and Anna dug into her pocket. She had $15 to spend today, and that included lunch. She looked at the price. One dollar would buy four rounds of skeeball. She decided to splurge.

"If you score 180 or above, you win a prize," Kenzie commented as she dug $1.00 out of her back pocket.

Anna eyed up the prizes. Mostly, they were small things like little rope bracelets and pieces of candy. She didn't really care if she won a prize, but she did like playing skeeball.

None of them won any prizes, but they all had fun. Then they decided to walk around and survey all the different food options that were available so they could make educated choices when it was time for lunch. Anna still favored the barbecued chicken, but she had to admit that the walking tacos looked good. And Jane's Diner had set up a little stand with their ice cream cones. Maybe she'd have that for dessert.

CHAPTER 12

"Anna!" Sparrow seemed so excited when she came running over to Anna at the festival. Fern followed, holding Anna's mother's hand.

"This looks so fun," said Sparrow. She looked at the row of games. "Can we play games now?"

"We'll play them soon," Anna promised. "Can I show you girls inside the gym first?"

Both girls nodded eagerly. On their way into the gym, Anna was able to introduce the girls to several of her gymnastics friends. As they entered the gym, Coach Cyndi was walking by with Mrs. Edgarson, the gym owner of Maple Hill Gymnastics. They saw Anna's family and stopped.

Anna introduced the two new foster children. Coach Cyndi knew that her family took in children regularly and was always eager to hear about them. She smiled and greeted the girls warmly, as did Mrs. Edgarson.

"Sparrow would like to start gymnastics classes," Anna's mom smiled as she spoke. "I'm working with her social worker to arrange it. I'm hoping she can start soon."

"That would be wonderful," said Coach Cyndi. "I can't wait to see her in the gym regularly." Sparrow smiled from ear to ear.

"In the meantime," said Mrs. Edgarson, "Go ahead and let the girls try out all the preschool gym equipment today. I'm sure they'll have fun!"

Anna and her parents led the two girls over to the bright, colorful preschool area. There were floor-level beams and beams a few inches off the ground. There were mini sets of rings, and small bars, as well as mini sets of uneven bars. In the corner, a large trampoline and a tumble track provided a place to run, jump, and flip.

Fern was so happy as she ran on the tumble track, jumping and laughing. Anna took Sparrow over to the beam. Sparrow got on, and Anna got on the beam next to her and showed her the proper way to walk across, toes pointed. She showed her how to walk backward. Sparrow seemed to be enjoying herself.

After the beam, Anna led Sparrow to a bar and showed her a pullover.

"Do you want to try doing a pullover?" she asked Sparrow.

"I'll try, but it looks a little hard," said Sparrow. "Can you help me?"

"Of course I'll help you!" Anna replied.

Sparrow kicked up, and Anna grabbed her feet and helped her over the bar. She helped Sparrow hold herself up for a moment.

"I did it!" said Sparrow. It needed some work, of course, but Anna felt proud that Sparrow was trying, and Anna was enjoying her role as a teacher.

There was a springboard set up next to a resi mat for the little ones to practice vault. Anna ran to the springboard, jumped, and landed with her feet together on the mat to show Sparrow what to do. Sparrow copied Anna. She ran, jumped, and landed. She fell on her first try but got up smiling and was ready to try it again. Anna felt like Sparrow was getting the hang of things quickly.

Sparrow wanted to try hanging on the little ring set in the gym, and Fern also came over to try. Anna's parents cheered the girls on as Anna lifted them each up to let them try hanging from the rings.

"Hey, they're pretty good!" Anna heard a voice behind her. She turned around to see Parker standing there. "Seriously," he said. "I don't know if I was that good my first time doing rings."

Anna introduced the girls to Parker, and he showed them some flips on the tumble track. Fern ran down the tumble track then and tried to do a flip, which ended up looking more like a forward roll. Then Anna showed them some different jumps—split jumps, tuck jumps, and straddle jumps.

"Are you getting some lunch?" asked Parker.

"Yeah, Kenzie was waiting for me," said Anna. "But you can join us."

"Go ahead out," said Anna's parents, "we'll stay here with the girls until they're ready for lunch."

Anna and Parker walked towards the exit of the preschool area.

"ANNA!" called Sparrow suddenly. Anna turned around to see Sparrow running up behind her with Fern following. "Don't leave! Play with us."

"Anna is going to have lunch with her friends," Anna's dad told the girls. "We'll play some more, and then get lunch before we watch Anna and her team do some gymnastics."

"I want to eat with Anna. I want to eat now," said Sparrow.

Anna looked from Sparrow to Fern with pleading eyes. She turned to Parker.

"Is it okay if the girls join us?" she asked.

"Sure," said Parker. "Why not?"

"Alright, you and Kenzie can eat with my family then, I guess. If that's okay." Anna couldn't bear to disappoint Sparrow and Fern. She had already grown fond of them, and she could see they liked her. She knew they had already experienced enough disappointment in their young lives.

Anna's family got in line with Parker and Kenzie for the barbecued chicken, which was what they all had decided on for lunch. The smell wafted through the air, and Anna's mouth watered as they patiently waited their turn.

"Let's get Boba tea after lunch," Kenzie suggested.

"Let's get it with lunch!" said Anna. "I saw they have a new honeydew flavor this year."

Later that night, after the girls were in bed, Anna pulled out her journal. It had been a good day, and she wanted to write about it for the memories. Even the gymnastics exhibition with her team had gone smoothly, and Anna had done all her skills with ease. She felt happy, remembering how excited Sparrow and Fern had been. Everything about the day had made the two girls happy, and that was one of the best parts for Anna. She wrote down everything she could remember, storing up the memories. If Sparrow and Fern went home someday, she would still have her memories in this journal.

CHAPTER 13

F riday night, Anna went to the gym for a special extra practice since her team was having their final meet before states the next day. Anna was excited because she felt like she had improved. Maybe her scores would go up at least a little.

"Are you ready for tomorrow?" asked Kenzie. "I hope I do well. The next time we'll compete after this is the state competition, and I really want to win medals there."

"I'm ready," said Suryea. Suryea always seemed ready for anything. She was talented and determined, and Anna admired that about her friend.

They started out with a meeting with Coach Cyndi.

"Girls," Coach Cyndi said, "Just a few reminders for tomorrow. The meet starts with warm-up at 9:00 a.m., so be sure you're there early. Also, don't forget your gym bags and your water bottles. I'm excited about our competition! Tonight, after warm-up, we'll start on bars and go through our routines as if it's a real meet."

"What event do we start on tomorrow?" asked Kenzie.

"Bars. That's why we're starting there tonight," smiled Coach Cyndi.

Anna felt like the practice went smoothly. She felt like she was more than ready for the next day. As she high-fived her teammates at the end of practice, she had a feeling that maybe tomorrow would be her day to win a medal.

"Get to bed early tonight," Anna's mother reminded her when she got home.

Anna opened the cupboard, searching for her usual nightly snack. "I will. Don't worry. Tomorrow is going to be a good competition, I think," she told her mom. She selected some beef jerky and sat down with a book to relax. The house was very quiet. Anna's mom was sorting some paperwork, and her dad was responding to an email. Sparrow and Fern were in bed, sleeping. Anna enjoyed her quiet evenings with her family—it gave her some refreshing downtime.

Anna made sure to write in her journal about the night's practice and her hopes for the meet the next day before she went to bed. By 9:30, she was tucked in under her fluffy bedding and well on her way to a good night's sleep.

"Momma!" Anna jerked awake. She glanced at her clock. It said 1:30 a.m. Why was she awake? She heard it again. Soft sobs from the bedroom next door and a child crying for their mother. Fern must be up like she was almost every night. Lately, Anna's mom had been awake nightly with Fern for hours, holding her and rocking her as she cried.

Just to make sure all was okay, Anna rolled out of bed and into her slippers. She quietly peeked into the bedroom next door.

It was dark except for the night light, and Fern was sobbing in her crib, crying for her mother. Sparrow lay in her own bed, fast asleep. Then Anna noticed her mom on the floor next to Fern's crib, fast asleep. Her poor mother, thought Anna. She must have come in to be with Fern and felt so exhausted that she was sleeping right through Fern's crying. And Fern and Sparrow would not be comforted by Anna's dad, even though he was always so kind to them. Anna thought it wouldn't be helpful to wake her dad up. The girls always wanted her mother when they were this upset.

Thinking quickly, Anna tiptoed over and pulled Fern from the crib. When she saw Anna, Fern immediately stopped sobbing so hard. Anna wrapped Fern in a blanket, and carried her gently to the rocking chair in their living room. She sat down and rocked Fern slowly, singing the songs her mom always sang. Slowly Fern settled, and the occasional sobs or cries of "Mama" quieted gradually until they stopped entirely. Anna just kept rocking and singing, watching the girl settle. Fern's eyes closed, and she began to fall asleep.

Anna wondered how long her mom sat there with Fern before putting her back in her crib. Anna didn't want to wake Fern, so she decided she would rock her for at least fifteen minutes longer. She was running out of songs to sing, so she began "You Are My Sunshine" for the third time.

It was now 3:00 a.m. according to the clock on the wall. It was 3:00 a.m., and in a few hours, she had to get up and go compete at the gymnastics competition. Her eyes felt droopy. Would her body be too tired tomorrow? Would she still do well?

Finally, it seemed that Fern was in a deep sleep, so Anna carried the child gently back to her crib. She laid her down tenderly and covered Fern with the blanket. Fern barely stirred and continued to sleep. Anna felt a sigh of relief.

She turned to leave the bedroom, then glanced down at her mom on the floor. She quietly walked into the hall and opened the linen closet, grabbing a spare blanket off the shelf. Without waking her mom, Anna covered her gently with the blanket and left the room. Everything was mostly quiet and peaceful now; she could hear her dad's light snoring from her parent's bedroom.

Anna was exhausted when she climbed back into bed. She didn't have time to worry about the meet the next day—she fell instantly asleep.

CHAPTER 14

When her alarm rang, Anna felt groggy, but she jumped out of bed and rushed into the kitchen for breakfast before she put on her competition leotard. Anna's mom smiled as she put a bacon, egg, and cheese sandwich in front of Anna. It was Anna's favorite breakfast before a competition. Sparrow and Fern were already dressed and watching cartoons in the living room.

"Thanks, Mom," said Anna, taking a bite.

"Anna, I was wondering something," her mom said. "Did you cover me with a blanket last night? I asked Dad already, and he said it wasn't him."

Anna then told the whole story of what had transpired in the night.

"Oh, Anna!" said her mom. "You have a meet today. You should have woken me or your father up! It's our job to take care of those situations, not yours. You're a child." Anna's mom walked over and gave her a big hug. "Thank you for caring about me, sweetie, but next time, please wake me up to handle things."

"I felt so bad," said Anna. "You've been up every single night."

"Anna, that's what I signed up for," her mom said. "It's really okay. I'm just glad we can show these girls some love and care."

Anna nodded and finished up the last of her sandwich. Her mom hugged her again when she stood up from the table.

"Anna, you're such a sweet daughter. I love you so much," her mom said. "You have a kind and compassionate heart, and that means a lot to me."

"Is everyone coming to my competition?" Anna asked.

"Yes," her mom said, "Dad ran out to water the garden, but he's ready to go. The little girls are ready. Hurry and put your leotard on! I'm ready to do your hair."

Anna went back to her bedroom to put on the Maple Hill Gymnastics competition leo. She loved the way she looked when she had her leotard on and her hair done, all ready for a meet. She felt excited when she looked in the mirror. Anna got dressed, then quickly checked her backpack to make sure everything she might need was inside.

She put in a pair of leggings and an extra shirt so she could change after the meet. Thankfully, this meet was at a community center in between her gym and the hosting gym, so it was only an hour and a half drive today. Anna pulled out her water bottle and went to fill it up in the kitchen before her mom started her hair.

Anna felt a few butterflies in her stomach when she checked into the meet an hour later. Fern and Sparrow had clung to her side, but her mom had persuaded them to let her go, telling the girls they would get to see Anna compete for the first time! Anna made her way to the mat, where Coach Cyndi was already waiting.

"Nice and early, as usual," Coach Cyndi smiled. "I can always count on you to be the first one here."

Anna saw Fern and Sparrow waving and waved back.

"How are the new girls doing?" asked Coach Cyndi. "They're adorable. It seems they like you already."

Anna nodded. "They really do, and I like them." She yawned, suddenly feeling a little tired from the night before.

"Yawning already? We didn't even warm up yet," Coach Cyndi said. "Did you get enough sleep?"

"Well. . " Anna hesitated, then told Coach Cyndi about the events of the night before.

"My mom would have preferred me to wake her or my dad up, I guess," she finished. "But my mom just looks so tired lately. And my dad tries to help, but it seems the girls always want my mom. I know they miss their own mom, so maybe that's why."

Coach Cyndi looked at Anna with a very thoughtful look, and she didn't speak for a few minutes.

"That was kind of you, Anna," she said at last. "I love the way your family, including you, shows real love to these kiddos."

Just then, Kenzie and Suryea and a couple of their other teammates walked over. "Did you see the team over there? They have like twenty girls on their team," Kenzie was saying.

"Must be a big gym," Suryea commented.

"Girls, start stretching," said Coach Cyndi.

Anna yawned again, put down her backpack, and joined the other girls in stretching. She hoped she would do well today, maybe even better than average.

CHAPTER 15

After introductions and the playing of the national anthem, Anna's team rotated to vault where they would start. Anna got in line to warm up her front handspring vault. Although in practice they often did the vault over the actual vaulting table to up-train, in competition the Xcel Silvers completed their front handspring vault over a mat stack as required.

Anna's first warm-up vault was okay, but she took a huge step when she landed. She knew that would be a deduction and was determined to do better on her next warm-up. She watched as Suryea ran and completed a front hand-spring vault that looked perfect. She felt as if all her teammates were doing better than she was.

She got in line for her second warm-up. This time, it seemed to go better, and she only took a tiny step.

"That was nice," said Coach Cyndi. "Do your vault like that, and you'll be happy with your score." Anna felt pleased.

It was time to begin. Nervously, Anna stood on the blue mat runway and presented to the judge. The judge was not smiling. Anna hoped she was more friendly than she appeared.

She ran, did her front handspring, and surprisingly stuck the landing! Not even a tiny step! Anna was thrilled as Coach Cyndi gave her a high-five, and she headed back for her second vault. She was glad that in girls' gymnastics competitions, they were able to do two vaults. The highest score was the one that counted. She had learned that in boys' gymnastics meets, they were only allowed one vault.

Anna's second vault went well too, although she did take a small step and felt like she arched her back too much. She figured they would count the score of her first vault. She sat down with her teammates to watch Suryea vault and wait for her score to appear on the screen.

Suryea's first vault was beautiful, but she did hop on the landing. As Suryea walked back to do her second vault, Anna saw her score flash up. It was an 8.9. Anna smiled broadly. This was a decent score for her—almost a 9!

She felt thrilled. Maybe by her state meet, she would be able to score over a 9.0 on vault. Anna glanced over towards the bleachers and saw her dad give her a thumbs up. Sparrow was waving. Fern was playing with some little toys her parents had brought along. Sitting through a gymnastics meet was long, so Anna's parents had planned ahead for the girls.

Soon Anna's team had moved to uneven bars. Anna hoped she would continue her good performance. Unfortunately, though, she landed short on her dismount and fell back, catching herself with her hand. This was a big deduction, and on bars, she only scored an 8.0. She actually felt lucky that the score wasn't even lower.

"Don't worry," Kenzie tried to console her. "I've messed up on bars a few times this year. You can still finish the rest of the meet well. Just focus on doing your best on beam now."

Anna nodded, but she didn't feel convinced. Sometimes after she made a mistake, it was hard to get her mind back in the game.

Unfortunately, on beam, she fell on her handstand. Anna was very disappointed in herself because she had not fallen all year on her handstand. When she got back up on the beam, Anna tried to stay tight and clean for the remainder of the routine, reminding herself to keep doing her best. It must have helped, because she still scored an 8.4 on beam, even with the fall.

Floor would be their final event that day. Anna was starting to feel tired, though. The initial adrenaline had worn off. Anna pulled her water bottle from the side of her backpack and took a long drink of water. She focused on going through the entire floor routine in her mind, the way she did before every event.

Anna's floor routine went okay, for the most part. It wasn't perfect, and she knew she had messed up by falling forward and touching her hand down to the floor on her second pass. That would be a deduction. She also had not kept her legs as tight as she knew she should have during her leaps. It wasn't the floor routine she had hoped to have that day, but it wasn't the worst floor routine she had ever done. Her score flashed up: 8.4. Not horrible, but not great. Again, average.

Anna cheered her teammates on and then added up the scores in her head as they prepared to go to the awards ceremony. The total all-around score was a 33.7. She had been hoping for a 34—at least she had gotten close. Anna had improved on vault, so she was thankful for that.

Today, Anna received a candygram from her family with a cake pop. It was so cute! The cake pop was purple with pink and yellow swirls and even some tiny frosting flowers. Whoever had decorated these cake pops had clearly spent time and care.

"These are adorable!" said Suryea when she also received one. "I don't think I've ever had a cake pop this beautifully decorated before."

"I agree," smiled Coach Cyndi. "Someone put some work into those. They look too good to eat!"

"I don't know about that," said Anna. "As soon as awards are over, I'm eating mine."

Just then, Anna felt a tap on her shoulder. She turned around to see Sparrow standing there. She also saw her mom approaching to take Sparrow back to her seat.

"Hi, Anna!" said Sparrow. "You did so good at gymnastics."

Anna grinned. "Thanks, Sparrow," she said.

"Sparrow, come now, back to our seats," Anna's mom took her hand. "We have to wait until awards are over. Then you can talk to Anna."

"But I want that," Sparrow said, suddenly pointing to the cake pop. "I want that."

"You already had one, sweetie," said Anna's mom. "Now come, let's sit back down."

"But I want another one. That was my first cake pop I ever had. I want one more," Sparrow persisted, standing there, unyielding.

"Please, Anna," Sparrow said again. "Can I have it?"

"Come, Sparrow," said Anna's mom again. "We'll get lunch as soon as the awards are finished.

"But I don't want lunch; I want a cake pop. They are so good!" Sparrow was persistent.

"Here, Sparrow," Anna said suddenly. "You can have it. It's fine."

"Anna, we got that for you," her mom protested. "You don't have to do that."

"No, I want to," said Anna.

Sparrow took the pop, squealed and jumped up and down, and finally followed Anna's mom back to their seats.

"Why'd you give it to her?" asked Kenzie. "She already had one. She was being greedy."

Anna sighed. "The thing is, Kenzie, she may have never had treats like that before now. I'm sure her life has been really hard. Even now, being in foster care can't be easy at all. Anyway, it's just a cake pop. I'll get another."

"They're sold out now though," Kenzie said. "That's what the girls next to me told me."

"Oh well." Anna did feel disappointed, but then she said, "I can make cake pops sometime, maybe." She didn't feel convinced that she'd ever make cake pops that beautiful, but there was no sense worrying about it. Awards were starting.

"Sssh, girls," said Coach Cyndi. "They're announcing the winners."

Anna was pleasantly surprised to hear her name called for a fifth-place medal on vault. She had not been expecting to get anything, so the award was a bonus!   Maybe if she kept improving, someday she'd get a first-place medal! She imagined standing on top of the podium, winning a first-place award—now that would be something.

CHAPTER 16

As a surprise after the meet, Anna's family and some of the other families from Maple Hill Gymnastics met at an arcade about ten minutes from where the meet was held. They ordered pizza and sodas first and then got tickets to enjoy some of the games. Anna's parents took Sparrow and Fern over to the games and rides for younger children. Anna smiled as she saw her dad gently helping Fern and Sparrow onto the mini merry-go-round. They looked happy!

"Who wants to play me in this virtual reality game?" asked Kenzie.

Anna eyed it up. "I don't know," she said hesitantly. "The sign says 'A Haunted Adventure'."

"Come on," said Kenzie. "Please. You need two people to play. You're basically going through an old haunted amusement park, including riding a roller coaster. You'll love it."

Anna wasn't sure, but she decided to try the VR ride with her friend. She sat in the seat and put the headset on her head.

She was shocked at how realistic the ride was. She screamed the first time she saw a ghost jump out, and she felt as if she was actually on the roller coaster. It turned out to be more fun than she had imagined and not as scary as she feared. She did find herself jumping in her seat a lot, though.

After that, they played a game where you stood to shoot baskets to see who could get the highest score. Anna was pretty good at this one, making five baskets in a row. Suryea was also an accurate aim, and her score was the second highest.

The girls then decided to try out some of the more old-school arcade games. After a while, Anna's dad came over and showed them a few of the classics, the ones he used to play. Anna enjoyed trying them all.

Anna went with her dad back over to where her mom was with Sparrow and Fern. The little girls were just finishing riding on mini cars. Sparrow and

Fern each grabbed one of Anna's hands when they saw her.

Sparrow pointed to the photo booth. "Can we get a picture taken?" she asked.

Anna's mom nodded, and the girls arranged themselves inside the photo booth, making sure all their faces were visible to the camera—Fern on one side, Sparrow on the other, and Anna in between. Anna's dad swiped the card to pay for the photo, and the timer began to count down from ten. All three smiled for the picture. They waited for it to print out.

Anna held it out for Sparrow and Fern to admire. "Look, that's all of us," said Sparrow.

Fern nodded and pointed at herself. Anna felt pleased with the portrait. She was glad that the machine had printed out three copies. One for each of them! Anna wanted to keep hers in her journal so that when she remembered Sparrow and Fern, she could always look back at this photo.

After that, Anna went back over with Kenzie and Suryea to play a three-person racing game. Anna found herself swerving all over the road.

"It's good you aren't driving age yet," Suryea laughed.

"I'll be a good driver by then," Anna protested.

Suryea finished the race in first place; Anna was second, and Kenzie was third.

"Time to go," Anna's mom said, coming up behind the three girls. "Dad has Sparrow and Fern over in the store area, picking out their prizes."

Anna had earned enough digital tokens at the arcade to choose between a couple pieces of candy or a tiny stuffed bird. She hesitated, going back and forth, and finally decided on the tiny stuffed bird so she could set it on her shelf in her bedroom.

"I got this ball," said Sparrow, opening her hand. Anna saw a ball filled with some type of slime. "Look," Sparrow continued. "It's squishy. Feel it."

Anna touched the soft ball and squished it down. Slowly it returned to its' original shape as a ball. It was soft and like Sparrow had said, "squishy".

"That's really neat," said Anna. She turned to Fern. "What did you get?" she asked.

Fern quietly held up a little bird stuffed animal, similar to Anna's.

Anna held up hers. "Look, we have matching birds," she said. "Isn't that fun?"

Fern nodded with a slight smile and hugged the bird to herself.

That night, Anna hung her new medal from vault on her medal holder in her bedroom. It had been a while, she thought, since she had hung up a new medal. She fingered it carefully. Would she get more medals at her state competition? Would next year be the year when she finally did well and got medals in every event? Imagine the feeling of standing at the very top of the podium as a winner! She had to try even harder at practice. Someday, she wanted to be exceptional instead of average.

CHAPTER 17

The next Tuesday night was Sparrow's first real gymnastics class at Maple Hill Gymnastics. Anna's mom had finally gotten approval from the agency, and Sparrow was all signed up and ready to go. Earlier that afternoon, when they were riding the bus, Sparrow had tapped Anna's back.

Anna had stopped her conversation with Erica. Turning around, she said, "What, Sparrow?"

"What will I wear to gymnastics tonight?" Sparrow asked eagerly. Anna saw that Sparrow had been drawing a picture. On her lap was an open school notebook. Sparrow had sketched a girl on the balance beam with a big smile across her face. Anna knew that Sparrow was excited to start gymnastics—she had been talking about it non-stop for the past few days.

"Hmmm," said Anna. "I actually think I have a couple leotards you can borrow from when I was around your age. Come over to my room when we get home."

"Really?" said Sparrow. "Oh, thank you, Anna. What color are they? Do they sparkle?"

Anna laughed. "I'll show you as soon as we get home," she promised.

When they arrived, Anna went back into her bedroom and opened her closet. She reached her hand up to her top shelf and pulled a storage container down. In that container were some gymnastics mementos she was saving, including favorite leotards that she had outgrown. She held them up, one by one, until she found two that she thought might fit Sparrow.

Anna set the leotards on her bed. Sparrow was still having a snack in the kitchen with Fern.

Anna sat for a moment, thinking. Then she unlocked her sewing closet and pulled out the linen fabric she had ordered as well as the dress pattern. She held up the fabric again, admiring it. What a good choice! Yes, as she compared it to the pattern, she felt more convinced than ever that it was the perfect combination.

"Anna?" She heard a knock.

Anna looked up. "Oh, Sparrow, come in." Sparrow came over to Anna's bed.

"What's that?" she asked, pointing at the fabric.

"Oh, this is so I can sew a dress for my gymnastics banquet," Anna explained. "Isn't it pretty?"

Sparrow fingered the edge of it softly and looked at it with admiring eyes. "It's beautiful," she said. She pointed to the pattern. "Is that what your dress will look like?"

"Yeah," said Anna. "Oh, there are the two leotards." She motioned toward the end of the bed.

Sparrow didn't move right away. "Can you make a dress for me too? And Fern?" she asked softly.

Anna looked at her and said, "Sure. Maybe this summer. I'll let you pick out the fabric yourself."

"I like that fabric," said Sparrow.

Anna set the fabric down and turned to the leotards. She held up a blue leotard with some sequins on the front.

"How about this one?" she asked Sparrow.

Sparrow looked at it for a while, then glanced at the other leotard on the bed, the one that was mostly white with red and blue sequins. She looked back and forth, from leo to leo.

"It's a hard choice," she said finally. "This is my first real gymnastics class ever. I think I'll wear that one." Sparrow pointed to the white one on the bed.

"Sure," Anna handed it to Sparrow. "You can wear the other one next week if you want. Why don't you take them both to your room?"

Sparrow picked up the blue leotard as well and ran to her room.

Anna picked up the pattern and fabric to put them back in her cupboard. She went over to the mirror first, holding the fabric up in front of her. It was still her favorite fabric ever. As she locked it in the cupboard, she thought about Sparrow and Fern. Should she make them dresses with it instead? Then she'd never get to wear it. And what would she wear for the banquet? Well, she thought, she didn't need to decide that day. She would think about it.

At Maple Hill Gymnastics that evening, Anna watched as her mom walked Sparrow over to her group and introduced her to Maggie, the instructor. Sparrow looked proud and happy in Anna's white leotard with her brown hair up high in a bun. Anna wished she could watch Sparrow's entire practice to see how she did, but she knew it was time to warm up with the team.

Between turns doing jumps on the tumble track, Anna watched Sparrow practicing pullovers with her class on a low bar. Sparrow looked like she was enjoying herself. Anna was happy for her!

At snack, the girls discussed the upcoming season of gymnastics and who would be moving on to Xcel Gold.

"Is anyone staying Silver?" asked Anna. "Besides me, I mean."

"Not me," said Suryea. "I can't wait to get to Gold. I'm tired of the Silver music. Also, I want to get to Platinum in a couple years."

"I'm going to repeat Silver," Sadie, a younger, newer girl to the team said.

Anna nodded. She wondered how it would be next season, not competing with Kenzie and Suryea anymore. She'd have to make new friends. Maybe someday she'd get to Gold.

Coach Cyndi came over just then. "Maggie said that your little foster sister loved gymnastics," she said to Anna. "She was pretty talented and fun to have in the class."

"She was excited," said Anna. "She likes to practice skills at home with me."

"I'm so glad she has the opportunity," said Coach Cyndi. Anna agreed. Seeing the foster children get to experience these types of opportunities always made her happy inside.

CHAPTER 18

It was finally the day of the Knoebels class trip. Anna was excited as she sat in her seat on the bus beside Erica. They had just arrived at the park, and the teacher was giving instructions. Anna had her string bag on already, just waiting to get permission to leave the bus and head for the park.

Anna's teacher finished, and they all exited the bus, lining up in a double line behind the teacher to walk to the ticketing booth, where they would each receive a wristband. Anna was glad her parents had paid the extra fee so that she could ride all the roller coasters. Those were her favorites, especially the Phoenix.

"Look," Erica pointed to the French fry stand. "Those are the home-cut fries that we split every year when my family comes here."

"We always get the pizza," said Anna. They passed a kiddie boat ride and a merry-go-round. "I think Sparrow and Fern would love this park," Anna said, "I hope they're still with us when we come as a family this summer."

"I like catching the rings on the merry-go-round," Anna heard a boy in front of her say. Anna agreed. She loved trying to catch the rings.

After they got their wristbands, Anna and Erica headed towards the log flume. It was already getting warm out, and both girls agreed it would be fun to start the day off with a nice, wet ride.

Anna loved the feeling of riding up the hills on the log flume and then the splash as you descended into the water. She and Erica got good and wet on the log flume. In fact, Anna had to try to wring some of the water out of her shorts.

"I didn't think we'd get quite that wet," Erica laughed. "Do you want to ride the Phoenix now?"

"The line is pretty long," said Anna. "Let's try the antique cars first, and then ride the Phoenix since they're next to each other."

After a ride on the antique cars and two rides on the Phoenix roller coaster, Anna and Erica went back towards the Haunted Mansion. Anna didn't usually love haunted attractions, but this haunted house was not too scary. Anna made sure to ride it every time she visited the park.

Two Haunted Mansion rides and three merry-go-round rides later, the girls made their way back to the pavilion, where they were all meeting for a hot dog lunch. So far it had been a good day, and Anna eagerly picked up a lemon-lime soda to go with her hot dog and apple slices. She was thirsty from all the walking around the park.

"Look at the boys. They're completely soaked!" a girl in Anna's class was saying.

Anna looked over. Indeed, the boys were dripping wet from head to toe. Anna knew they couldn't have gotten that wet from the log flume. Maybe they had stood underneath the Skloosh water ride to be splashed by a huge deluge of water when it came down the hill!

When they finished their lunch, Anna and Erica went down to the stream by the pavilion. They sat by the edge of the stream and watched it go by.

"Are you looking forward to summer?" asked Erica thoughtfully. "I am. I'm tired of schoolwork, and I want to go visit my aunt in New York."

"How long will you be gone this year?" asked Anna.

"Only a week," Erica said. "She's taking us to Niagara Falls, so that should be fun."

"I guess I'm looking forward to summer. I'll still be in the Xcel Silver training group at gymnastics. Most of my friends are moving to Gold," Anna said.

"Oh," said Erica. "I can see how that would be frustrating. Do you still like gymnastics?"

"Yes, yes," Anna said quickly. "I love it."

Erica took her shoes and socks off and slid her feet into the cool water. "We'll be in middle school in the fall," she said. "That's weird. I used to think kids in middle school were so old."

"Me too," Anna agreed. "But I don't feel that old now. I hope it's not too hard in middle school. I'm worried about being late to class or forgetting something."

They sat for a long time, just enjoying the rushing of the creek across the stones and the glinting of the sun on the water. Then Anna stood up. "We should go back and ride more rides while we still have time," she said.

Erica took her feet from the stream. "Yeah, you're right. I wanted to ride the boats and other roller coasters. Let's get going."

CHAPTER 19

Anna's mom was outside with the girls after dinner, and Anna wandered out to play with them since she didn't have gymnastics. Sparrow was playing with Fern in the sandbox.

"Nice castle," said Anna, walking over. She grabbed a bucket and helped them add two more towers.

"Let's add three more on the other side," Sparrow suggested. Anna nodded and dug more sand into the bucket.

When they had finished building, Anna's mom called to her, "Anna, come here for a few minutes."

Anna left the girls digging in the sand and walked over to where her mom was squatting, pulling some weeds out of last year's flower bed.

"What, Mom?" asked Anna.

Anna's mom pulled another weed and threw it to the side. "Anna," her mom spoke softly. "I got a call from Mrs. Lim today from the agency."

Anna's heart sank. She had a feeling this wasn't good.

"They've located Sparrow and Fern's aunt, and she's willing to take them in. She's a relative, so as long as the background checks come back clear and the home inspection and everything else is good, they'll be moving to live with her in a few weeks."

"Oh," Anna felt a little stunned, but she had always known this might happen. If a suitable relative could be found, kinship care for foster children was preferred. Still, she didn't know what to say. It felt so sudden.

"I'm sorry, Anna," her mom spoke softly. "I know you love the girls, and they've adjusted well to living here. But we have to also want what's best for them."

Anna sighed. "I know," she said, watching Sparrow and Fern, who were now racing on some plasma cars on the patio. "So two or three weeks?"

"Something like that, according to the agency," her mom confirmed.

Anna didn't say anything else. She went to her room and plopped on her bed, staring at the ceiling for a long time. In one sense, she should be used to this. It happened every time. Her family took in foster children, cared for them the best they could, and eventually those foster children moved on. That was life, whether she liked it or not.

Anna pulled out her journal and pondered what to write. There was so much going through her mind. She had probably three weeks left with Sparrow and Fern—she needed to make the most of it. Anna had a sudden thought. She went to her sewing cupboard, unlocked it, and pulled out the beautiful linen fabric she had ordered with the yellow and purple flowers. She had three weeks. That was enough time to sew matching dresses for the two girls before they left. Then, they would have something tangible to take with them to their next home to remember her by.

Later that evening, Anna called Sparrow and Fern into her room and pulled up sewing patterns for children's spring dresses on her Chromebook.

"I'm going to sew you each a dress with this fabric," Anna said, holding it up. Fern fingered it softly, smiling but not saying a word.

"Yay!" said Sparrow. "When will they be ready so we can wear them?"

Anna laughed, "That will take a couple weeks, Sparrow. I still have to order the pattern. Then it will take me some time to sew the dresses!"

"Oh," Sparrow replied. She hesitated, then asked, "Could we wear them to your gymnastics banquet?"

Anna wasn't sure how to respond. Her gymnastics banquet was in about three weeks, and maybe the girls wouldn't be here any longer. However, Sparrow and Fern had no idea that they would be moving to another home. No one had told them yet; that was up to their social worker and the agency.

"Maybe you can wear them even sooner than that!" Anna said, "I'll try to get them sewn as fast as I can."

"Can you teach me to sew?" asked Sparrow.

"That takes a long time to learn,' said Anna. "And a lot of practice. My grandma taught me, but at the beginning I made a lot of mistakes."

Anna remembered the first time she had sewn her own pillowcase and how happy she had been. She still had that pillowcase, even though it was worn out. She felt such a sense of accomplishment when she finished her first sewing project. Anna really wished she had the time to teach Sparrow to sew, but she knew that she didn't. She was running out of time with Sparrow.

Sparrow selected a simple sundress pattern, one that would be easy for Anna to sew. She knew both girls would look adorable in their dresses, and she ordered the pattern right away. Anna couldn't wait to start sewing.

CHAPTER 20

It was a fun practice night at Maple Hill Gymnastics. Every so often, Coach Cyndi would declare a fun night where the team would do various games and activities instead of their usual practice routine. Anna and her teammates loved fun nights because they added some variety and excitement to practice. The Xcel Golds and Level 3s, 4s, and 5s were also included. Coach Cyndi, Coach Michelle, and Coach Jennifer split them up into teams.

"First," said Coach Cyndi, "we'll be having a back tuck contest for anyone who can do a back tuck. Whoever can land the most back tucks in a row is the winner for their team."

Anna decided to try participating even though she was pretty sure she couldn't land a back tuck. When it was her turn, she jumped high, did a tuck, but landed on her knees on the mat. She laughed because it had been fun anyway. She realized that she wasn't actually that far from doing a back tuck, and with more practice, she would probably be able to land it!

The next contest was to see how far each gymnast was able to walk on their hands in a handstand. The girls all lined up. When Coach Michelle called "Start", they began walking across the floor. Anna was good at handstand walks. She made it across the floor with no problem, but when she turned around to go back the other way, she fell down. She stood up to see who would win the contest. A girl named Bryn, who was Xcel Gold, walked across the mat three and a half times before she finally fell! Anna was glad that Bryn was on her team!

After that, the girls went to beam for a beam hop contest. They would hop across the beam and see who could stay on the beam the longest. Anna was excited when it was her turn. She mounted the beam and carefully started out, doing small hops across the beam. She made it across once, twice, and three times and kept going. Anna was on a roll! She didn't fall until halfway through her seventh time across the beam.

Everyone clapped! "That's our record so far," announced Coach Michelle. "Anna has made it six and a half times across the beam!"

Anna watched in anticipation as the next girls took their places on the beam and began to hop across. Kenzie was doing pretty well. She was at five times, going on six. Oops! She fell off right as she turned! Anna was still in the lead.

"And our winner is Anna!" Coach Cyndi announced. "Her team will receive 100 points for that contest!"

Anna's team cheered and gathered around her, giving her high fives and hugs. She loved the feeling of winning for her team. She felt important, like what she had done had added value. As they took a break and went to get their snacks from their cubbies, Anna pondered how it had felt to win for her team. Good. It had felt good. Winning felt a lot better than being average. She wished she was winning more often.

Anna turned to a girl sitting near her, Dana. She knew Dana had won a lot of medals, especially on the uneven bars. Dana was really good at bars;

Anna admired the way she flew across the bars and soared in her dismounts.

"Hey, Dana," Anna said suddenly. "What's it like when you win first place in a gymnastics competition?"

Dana was in the middle of dipping a pretzel in hazelnut dip, so she took a minute to answer.

"Really great," she said finally. "I mean, I always know that I still have things I can improve on. But winning feels amazing. Just standing up there, on top of the podium, knowing I did it." Dana took a bite of her pretzel. "And I know I helped our team score too," she added.

Anna nodded. "That's true," she said. The Xcel Silvers had won some team awards, but Anna was pretty certain her scores had not contributed to the team score. Her scores were too low. The highest three scores on each individual event were the ones that counted towards team awards in gymnastics competitions.

"I used to really just like getting the medals," Dana continued, "But now I have a lot of medals, so it's not really about the medals anymore. I'm happier if I can see that I did better and that my score improved."

Anna realized that she also cared more about whether her score had improved or not, but it was still nice to receive a medal. Maybe she valued them more because she hadn't won very many.

As Anna was walking over to the bars to continue their fun practice, Coach Cyndi caught up with her.

"I heard you talking with Dana," she said. "You know, Anna, you've been working really hard this year, and you're improving all the time. I'd say you're going to have an excellent season next year. You'll probably surprise yourself at how well you do."

Anna sighed. "I'll be repeating Silver when all my friends are going to Gold," she said.

"Everyone moves at their own pace, Anna. Trust me, you are going to have a great season if you keep working as hard as you have been," Coach Cyndi assured her.

"I hope so," said Anna a bit reluctantly. "It would be nice to win sometimes."

Coach Cyndi paused and placed her hand on the lower bar. "There are other ways to win, Anna," she said finally.

"What do you mean?" Anna asked.

"Someday, you won't be competing in gymnastics anymore. Don't get me wrong; it's wonderful to win medals in gymnastics, but there are other more important things in life. School, for example. You take your education with you your entire life, Anna. So if you're doing your best in school and learning, you're winning!" Coach Cyndi continued, "Your character also matters a lot more than your gymnastics scores. A person who has character, who is kind, who is full of integrity will go far in life, even if their gymnastics scores are average."

Anna nodded. She understood what Coach Cyndi was saying, but right now she just wished she could win at gymnastics.

Chapter 21

It was 10:00 p.m., and Anna was putting the finishing touches on the girls' dresses. Tomorrow was the day that Sparrow and Fern were leaving to go live with their aunt. It was also the day of Anna's gymnastics banquet. Anna had been hoping the girls would leave after the banquet, but Mrs. Lim had said that their aunt had met all the requirements and was ready to take Sparrow and Fern home with her as soon as possible.

Anna held up Sparrow's sundress. It had turned out just perfect. She was proud of the job she had done sewing these dresses. The girls could try them on tomorrow before Mrs. Lim from the agency arrived. In fact, they could wear these dresses home to live with their aunt. Fern's dress was tiny and adorable.

Anna laid them side by side on the bed and looked at them for a long time.

Finally, she started putting her sewing things back into the cupboard. As she did, it occurred to her that she had not decided what she would be wearing to the banquet tomorrow. She stopped and walked over to her closet. She pulled out a few dresses. There was the white dress she had worn to a family wedding last year. It looked like it would still fit. Or maybe she should wear the green dress that her mom bought her online last spring for Easter. She hesitated and decided to go with the white one if it still fit.

Anna's mom knocked. "Time for bed, sweetie," she said softly, entering the room.

Anna finished putting her stuff away. Her mom looked at the dresses on the bed.

"Those are gorgeous, Anna!' her mom said admiringly. "The girls will be so thrilled. I'm proud of you. You know, you didn't have to use your fabric to sew dresses for Sparrow and Fern, but you did it because you have a kind heart." She gave Anna a quick hug.

"I love the way they turned out," Anna said, hanging each one on a hanger. "I guess I'll wear the white dress to the banquet tomorrow night." She motioned towards the dress she had draped over her desk chair.

"Good choice. You'll look stunning," her mom said. "Do you want to go shopping for something different after the girls leave tomorrow afternoon? I'd be happy to buy you a new dress for your banquet if you'd like."

Anna shook her head, knowing she wouldn't be in the mood for shopping after losing Sparrow and Fern. "Nah, I won't be getting any awards at the banquet anyway."

"Anna, now don't say that," her mom protested.

"It's true, Mom," Anna said. "You remember. They give out awards for the highest scores on each event, and they also present the Amazing Gymnast Award. Last year Carissa Linden got that award—she's the level 10 that finished in fifth place at nationals and is competing in college now. No one is giving awards to an average Xcel Silver. And that's fine," she finished a little sadly.

Anna's mom sighed. "Well, I'm sure you'll still have a good time with your friends."

"I know," Anna said. "I guess I'll go to bed now. It's late."

The next day, Anna spent the morning helping her mom and the girls get all their things together. Anna's parents had not told them until that morning that they would be leaving for their aunt's house. The social worker said it was best that way. Anna's mom had washed, dried, and folded the girls' clothing neatly. The girls had brand new luggage ready to pack for their aunt's house.

"What is our aunt like?" asked Sparrow.

"I don't know; I've never met her," Anna said honestly. "I'm sure she's nice, though. Just think, she really wanted you to come live with her." Anna really hoped their aunt was truly kind and nice and good.

"Will I ever get to do gymnastics again?" asked Sparrow. "Do you want your leotards back?" She held up the white one with the red and blue sparkles.

Anna shook her head. "No, keep them. I'm hoping you get to do gymnastics again sometime. And even if you can't go to classes, you can still put your leotard on and practice at home. Never stop practicing!" Anna encouraged her.

When they had finished a lot of the packing, Anna led the two little girls into her bedroom.

"Close your eyes," she said. "I have a surprise for you!"

The girls covered their faces with their hands, and Anna told them not to peek. She held up the two dresses and said, "Open your eyes now!"

The two girls stared with wide eyes at the dresses as Anna handed one to each of them.

"Surprise!" she said. "I made you each a dress from my special fabric. Do you like them?"

Sparrow fingered the dress thoughtfully with big eyes. Finally, she looked up and smiled. "I love it," She said. "Can I wear it now, Anna?"

"Of course!" Anna said. "Go put it on! I hope it fits well! How about you, Fern? Do you like it?"

Fern just nodded with large eyes. She followed Sparrow into the bedroom to try on her dress.

When the girls came back out, Anna was thrilled to see that the dresses fit perfectly. The girls twirled around in them, laughing. Anna's heart felt happy inside. She hoped that Sparrow and Fern would remember her whenever they wore these dresses. She would really miss them. It would be hard to say goodbye.

CHAPTER 22

The banquet hall was in a large barn that had been converted into a rustic but gorgeous venue. Weddings and other formal events were often hosted there, and Maple Hill Gymnastics held the annual banquet in this hall every spring. Anna smiled in spite of her heavy heart as she and her parents walked in, and she saw the lights hanging from the rafters and the spring flowers on each table.

"Welcome!" Coach Cyndi greeted her at the door. She shook hands with Anna's parents. Anna saw a questioning look in her eyes and knew she was probably wondering where Fern and Sparrow were. However, maybe Coach Cyndi figured it out because she didn't ask.

"So happy to see you!" Mrs. Edgarson smiled warmly. Anna knew all the staff worked hard to make the banquet a memorable experience each year.

Anna sat down at their assigned table between her parents. She was happy to see that Kenzie's family would be sitting across from them when they arrived. As they waited, Anna thought back to her goodbyes with Sparrow and Fern. It had been too fast. Mrs. Lim had arrived, and within ten minutes the girls were gone—off to their new home, wearing their special dresses.

Anna willed herself to stop thinking about it. These things happened regularly, she reminded herself. Children came into her home, and children left. It was a part of life as a foster family.

When Kenzie arrived, the two girls went to get some appetizers.

"Oh look, they have pickles on a stick," said Kenzie. "I love those. I was hoping they'd have them again each year."

Anna laughed and stabbed some cheese and pepperoni with her toothpick. "I don't know why you like those so much."

"Who do you think will get the Amazing Gymnast Award this year?" asked Kenzie.

Anna looked thoughtful. "Maybe Dana. She has had a really great season so far. Who do you think?"

"I'm really not sure. Stella qualified for nationals, so maybe her," Kenzie said. "Or if they pick from the younger levels, Katie went up two levels and scored pretty high. Remember, though, they don't always choose the highest-scoring gymnast. Two years ago Rachel received the award because she worked so hard to come back after her knee injury. She didn't even compete that year. But she still got the Amazing Gymnast Award."

"It's probably hard to decide," said Anna. "There are so many great gymnasts in Maple Hill. They could pick boys too, and I know a couple of the older boys are doing well."

Kenzie nodded, and the two girls walked over to get drinks.

"Boo!" Suryea surprised them from behind.

"You're lucky I didn't have a drink in my hand," said Kenzie. "I would have spilled it!"

"Where are your little foster sisters?" asked Suryea as she poured herself a lemonade. "I didn't see them at our table, and I thought maybe they were with you."

"They went to live with their aunt," said Anna. "Just today, actually."

"Oh wow," said Suryea. "For good?"

"Probably. . as long as it goes okay," Anna replied.

"Sorry," said Suryea. "I know you really liked them."

"Don't worry," Anna felt a little like she might cry, but she wanted to keep the occasion happy. "It happens all the time when your family has foster children. You just get used to it." She didn't feel used to it at the moment. Anna took a long, slow drink of her lemonade to calm herself down.

"Did you see Coach Michelle's dress?" Kenzie changed the subject, and Anna was thankful. "It's so pretty!"

"I know. I love it," said Suryea. "It's the perfect color of red for her."

Pretty soon, the meal was ready to be served. Anna enjoyed the flavorful salad, pasta, and chicken bites.

The food was always fresh and good, she thought as she buttered another roll. Soon it would be time for the coaches' speeches and the awards. And after that, she was looking forward to the chocolate cake she had seen on the dessert table.

CHAPTER 23

The first set of awards was for the three highest scores on each event for DP girls and for Xcel girls. Anna clapped loudly when Kenzie and Suryea both received an award for a top score—Kenzie on beam and Suryea on vault. She was proud of her friends and knew they worked hard.

After that, the boys' team also awarded certificates for the top three scores on each event for compulsory boys and for optional boys. The boys' team cheered super loudly for their teammates. Anna thought the boys always seemed fun and boisterous.

The coaches then came up, and each gave a short speech. Mostly, they thanked the gymnasts and their parents for a terrific season. They also thanked

Mrs. Edgarson for doing a good job running the gym and helping them succeed in their coaching roles.

"These speeches are too long," whispered Kenzie.

Anna smiled. "I know," she said. "But soon we'll hear who won the Amazing Gymnast Award."

The Amazing Gymnast Award was legendary at Maple Hill Gymnastics. A trophy and medal were awarded to one of the gymnasts every season. It was considered one of the highest honors a gymnast at Maple Hill could receive, and was presented by Mrs. Edgarson herself.

Often, the award went to an upper-level gymnast who had performed well and was headed off to college. Sometimes the award was given to a gymnast who was exceptionally hard-working or showed outstanding character or a gymnast who had overcome challenges. It gave the gymnasts something to work towards.

Finally, Mrs. Edgarson stood up. Anna eyed the gleaming trophy on the table behind her. Mrs. Edgarson picked up the microphone and began to speak.

"This year, I am pleased to once again present our Amazing Gymnast Award here at Maple Hill Gymnastics," she began. "As you all know, this award goes to a gymnast who embodies the qualities we admire here such as respect, kindness, hard work, and determination. The Amazing Gymnast goes to a gymnast who is someone we want our other gymnasts to emulate—someone we should all look up to."

Everyone clapped as if on cue, and Mrs. Edgarson paused. "For this year's award, I'm going to handle things a little differently. I'd like Coach Cyndi to come up and speak," she said. Anna was very surprised. Coach Cyndi was an Xcel coach. Could one of her friends be getting the award this year?

"Hello, all," Coach Cyndi spoke into the microphone. "I actually wanted to take some time tonight to talk about my own life." She paused and looked around the room. "Most of you don't know this, but as a child, I grew up in a difficult situation. For a while," she said, "I was actually in a foster home, away from my family."

Anna was shocked. She had no idea Coach Cyndi had once been a foster child. A foster child like Reese, Sparrow, and Fern. Wow, she thought. But she was also surprised that Coach Cyndi was sharing this now.

"And I was moved to three different foster families along the way," Coach Cyndi continued. "The first two were a bit rough. But the third family changed my life in a positive way. They helped me in school, played with me, took me on family trips, and even introduced me to gymnastics. For their kindness, I'm forever grateful." Coach Cyndi seemed like she was fighting back tears. Anna was caught up in her speech.

"So, tonight, I want to share that we have a gymnast in our own gym whose family does for their foster children what my third foster family did for me. They take them in and show them love, kindness, and care. This family changes lives—I know they do. But this gymnast from our gym is a big part of that." Coach Cyndi continued, "As her coach, I've watched this girl make many personal sacrifices out of love for the foster children her family is caring for. In short, I've seen this gymnast excel in becoming an amazing, loving, and caring foster sister to these children. I've seen this gymnast do very well in life. Honestly, this hard-working gymnast probably gets what most people would consider 'average' scores at her meets, but she's way more than her scores. She improves a little bit more every day!"

Anna's heart had stopped beating. She couldn't believe what she was hearing. She felt like she was in another surreal world. Mrs. Edgarson came back up and took the microphone.

"This year, we are awarding the Amazing Gymnast Award to a gymnast who works hard in the gym, giving her best effort. This is a gymnast who shows kindness, care, and diligence to her teammates, her family, and those in need. We are convinced that she will be successful not just in the gym but in life. I am proud to present this year's Amazing Gymnast Award to Anna Maddox." Mrs. Edgarson concluded, holding out the trophy. "Anna, please come up to receive your award."

Anna couldn't believe that all this was happening as she walked slowly towards the front of the banquet hall. She would never forget this day. In her mind flashed Sparrow and Fern in their new dresses, and she wished they could be there with her now. All the foster children were brave and amazing!

She slowly reached the front. Anna stood still as Mrs. Edgarson put the medal around her neck. At that moment, Anna knew that if she kept working diligently, she was sure to succeed. Still in shock, Anna took the trophy in her hands. Everyone clapped and cheered. Anna realized that this is what it felt like to win. Anna wasn't average. Anna was amazing!

Book #6--Rory's Return

Don't Miss Book #6 in The Gymnasts of Maple Hill Series — *Rory's Return*!

- **Chapter 1**

Rory slowly opened the heavy front door and walked into the lobby of Maple Hill Gymnastics. It was early that morning in late summer, and the gym was still quiet. Rory had asked to be dropped off early—she wanted to take a few minutes to get used to being back in the gym.

She stood in the lobby for a moment, looking at the banners hanging from the previous season. Angelina had won first place at the state meet in Level 6. Rory wondered if she would have placed in Level 6 if she had competed this past year. She glanced into the gym and saw the banner still hanging from the year she had won the all-around at states in Level 4.

Rory noticed that Tyree had won medals at regionals as she looked at his smiling face on another banner. It didn't really feel like she'd been gone a whole year, and yet she had.

Mrs. Winters, who usually worked the front desk, wasn't at her post to welcome Rory. Yet Rory knew they were expecting her that day, so she should probably just go into the gym. Her mom had offered to come in with her, but Rory had told her that she was 12 now, so she could manage on her own.

Rory had managed on her own a lot over the last year. Her mind flashed back to her last day in the gym. She had just finished Level 5 and started training with the Level 6 group. But that weekend, her parents shared some scary and hard news. Her mom, whom she loved more than anything, had been diagnosed with cancer.

Rory remembered how she had cried in her bedroom the first night after her parents had gently shared the news with her. Rory's mom had shared that her cancer was highly treatable and that the doctors were sure she would be alright after chemotherapy and radiation treatments. But Rory had been so scared. That was when she decided to quit gymnastics to stay home and help her mom.

It had been a long year, but things were better now. A few weeks ago, Rory had gone with her mom when she finished the final cancer treatment and rang the bell. Her mom was officially in remission! The doctors had declared her mother cancer-free. It had been a joyous day for Rory's family.

Rory walked into the gym slowly, looking around at the familiar equipment. Would she still be able to do all her skills? Would she have a lot to relearn?

"Rory!" she heard a familiar voice. It was Coach Michelle, coming towards her. She walked over to Rory quickly and gave her a big hug. "I'm so glad you're back! It's wonderful to see you. I told the team girls, and they are all so excited to see you today."

It was almost comforting for Rory to hear Coach Michelle's voice. She felt like she had stepped back in time, before this past year. It felt normal and good to be speaking with her coach.

"What training group will I be in?" she asked.

"You'll be with the girls who are training for Level 6!" said Coach Michelle. "Coach Tina will be working with you today."

Rory hesitated. "But I haven't done any gymnastics in over a year. What if I can't do my skills anymore?"

"You'd be surprised how much muscle memory kicks in," Coach Michelle spoke confidently. "I'm sure you'll be a little rusty, but I believe you'll catch up to the other girls in no time. You were always a hard worker, and I have confidence that you can do this."

"Where should I put my backpack and water bottle?" asked Rory, feeling sure her old cubby had been reassigned.

Coach Michelle led her over to the cubby area and showed her a new cubby with her name already on it. They had obviously prepared for Rory's return to the gym, and that made her feel good inside. She hadn't been sure she wanted to come back to gymnastics.

Almost reading her mind, Coach Michelle asked, "What made you decide to come back?"

Rory sighed. "My mom encouraged me to try gymnastics again." Rory's mom had been adamant that it was time for Rory to move on with her life and do things she enjoyed. In some ways, their entire family had been stuck in survival mode for the past year. But Rory's mom had insisted that this summer things would change.

"That's wonderful. How do you feel about coming back?" asked Coach Michelle.

"I really don't know yet," Rory replied honestly. In a way, it felt like coming home to something warm and familiar. Yet, in another way, she felt like a stranger at the gym now.

Rory pulled off her sweatshirt and eyed up her blue and purple leotard and black bar shorts. She was glad that this leo still fit. Her mom had said she could order a few new ones to replace the leos she had outgrown over the past year. Rory was excited to choose some new leotards.

Girls were starting to arrive. It was time to head over to the floor and warm up. This was it; time to see if she still was the same Rory who had been so good at gymnastics just over a year ago.

ABOUT THE AUTHOR

Jennifer Chandler participated in recreational gymnastics as a child, and two of her children are competitive gymnasts. Jennifer has enjoyed researching the sport and learning more about it through her years of involvement.

Jennifer's goal in the Gymnasts of Maple Hill Series is to write books that young readers enjoy, that accurately portray the sport of gymnastics, and that also depict the characters as real people with a variety of interests, hopes and dreams.

Jennifer has a Bachelor of Science degree. She particularly enjoyed her studies in history and education. Her hobbies are reading, writing, walking, watching her children do gymnastics, and spending time with her family.

Follow **www.facebook.com/gymnastsofmh/** to learn more about new releases and other promotions!

ALSO BY

Read all of the gymnastics stories in The Gymnasts of Maple Hill Book Series!

Book 1— *Preslie Perseveres*

Book 2—*Charlotte's Challenges*

Book 3— *Dana's Decision*

Book 4—*Skylar's Summer*

Book 5—*Average Anna*

Book 6—*Rory's Return*

Made in the USA
Las Vegas, NV
04 February 2024

85306972R00079